Joy,
The Dancing Spirit of Love
Surrounding You

Beverly Elaine Eanes

Paulist Press
New York/Mahwah, New Jersey

The Publisher gratefully acknowledges use of the following: the poem "Little and Large" by James J. Overholt in *From Tiny Beginnings*, copyright 1987. Used with permission of Brethren Press, Elgin, Illinois. *The Be (Happy) Attitudes* by Robert Schuller, copyright 1985, Word, Inc., Dallas, Texas. All rights reserved.

Cover/book design and interior illustrations by Nicholas T. Markell.

Library of Congress Cataloging-in-Publication Data

Eanes, Beverly Elaine.
    Joy: the dancing spirit of love surrounding you / by Beverly Elaine Eanes.
        p.   cm.—(Illuminations series)
    Includes bibliographical references.
    ISBN 0-8091-3560-4
    1. Joy—Religious aspects—Christianity. 2. Christian life. I. Title. II. Series: IlluminationBooks.
BV4647.J68E26   1995
241.4—dc20   94–49034
                                          CIP

Published by Paulist Press
997 Macarthur Boulevard
Mahwah, New Jersey 07430

Printed and bound in the
United States of America

Contents

To:
The images of God
I've experienced through

Family and Friends
my granddaughter, Chloe,
...a special joy

moments with others,
however fleeting
the wonders of nature
the beauty of the arts

JOYs All

in loving appreciation

IlluminationBooks
A Foreword

*I*lluminationBooks bring to light wonderful ideas, helpful information, and sound spirituality in concise, illustrative, readable, and eminently practical works on topics of current concern. Learning from stress; interior peace; personal prayer; biblical awareness; walking with others in darkness; appreciating the love already in our lives; spiritual discernment; uncovering helpful psychological antidotes for our tendency to worry too much at times; and important guides to improving interpersonal relations, are only several of the areas which will be covered in this series.

The goal of each IlluminationBook, then, is to provide great ideas, helpful steps, and needed inspiration in small volumes. Each book offers a new beginning for the reader to explore possibilities and embrace practicalities which can be employed in everyday life.

In today's busy and anxious world, Illumination-Books are meant to provide a source of support—without requiring an inordinate amount of time or prior preparation. Each small work stands on its own. Hopefully, the information provided not only will be nourishing in itself but also will encourage further exploration in the area.

One is obviously never done learning. With every morsel of wisdom each of these books provides, the goal is to keep the process of seeking knowledge ongoing even during busy times, when sitting down with a larger work is impossible or undesirable.

However, more than information (as valuable as it is), at the base of each work in the series is a deep sense of *hope* that is based on a belief in the beautiful statement made by Jesus to his disciples and in turn to us: "You are my friends" (Jn 15:15).

As "friends of God" we must seek the presence of the Lord in ourselves, in others, in silence and solitude, in nature, and in daily situations. IlluminationBooks are designed to provide implicit and explicit opportunities to appreciate this reality in new ways. So, it is in this spirit that this book and the other ones in the series are offered to you.

–Robert J. Wicks
General Editor, IlluminationBooks

Dancing Spirit

Dancing spirit
  Free
    As the breeze
That rustles
The leaves
And sets the trees
  Soaring,
    dipping,
      Waving,
  Reaching
    Toward Heaven.
As wind
  Circling the earth,
    Rolling the waves,
      Leaping the rocks,
        Splashing the streams.
A flame within
  Shining
  As radiant light
On a countenance
  Reflecting
    God's Love.
        —Beverly Elaine Eanes

Introduction

Pure Joy
(Receiving the Love
All Around You)

*E*ven the largest mammals on our
planet can be seen frolicking in the
sea. Whales leap and roll, and just
before they disappear beneath the surface of the
water they wave their flukes or tails. They seem
to be playing for their own enjoyment as well as
displaying their fun for the humans who are
watching them enthralled. It reminds us of God's
delight in all that he has created. And, is it not
for our delight as well...the myriad display of
color as fall beckons the trees to turn their leaves
to jeweled fire, or the melodic trill of a bird call-
ing to its mate? "Then shall all the trees of the

wood sing for joy before the Lord" (Psalm 96:12-13, Revised Standard Version [RSV]).

And, all the while, sun and shadow, wind and rain dance across meadow and wood. "The clouds are his chariots. He rides upon the wings of the wind." (Psalm 104:3, Living Bible [LB]).

But sunlight does not always shine and colors fade all too soon. Into each of our lives roll the cloudy days of sorrow and pain...the 'rain on our parade.' Our tears flow in unison with the rain, blurring the grace which flows all around us. David also knew pain and sorrow, but he was finally able to "dance before the Lord with all his might" (2 Samuel 6:14, RSV).

The fullness of joy has many facets, including: faith and hope; play and laughter; creativity and imagination; exploration and discovery; rapture and enthusiasm; bliss and peace. Expanded joy can include pain and sorrow, loss and grief.

God is with us in our dance of joy as well as in our triumph over despair. Are we "ready to be flexible—to move, to dance, to be prepared for healing wherever it comes from, and to participate in it?"[1]

We are *creative* beings fashioned in the image of our creator. We are, therefore, capable of letting go and *healing* the hurts which bind us, transforming our fear and sorrow, freeing our *faith* to enjoy the pleasures surrounding us here and *now*. Rising above the deepest darkness, we are able to *share* the joy in remembered play as God delights in us.

The Lord will take delight in you,
and in his love he will give you new life.
He will sing and be joyful over you,
as joyful as people at a festival
(Zeph. 3:17, Good News Bible [GNB]).

Joy is:

the wonder of a baby's
first snow
looking out...
reaching, smiling
as the slippery white crystals
glide against the glass

...enraptured joy!

Joy is:

The April tulip magnolia
blooming again in July
happening upon the
creamy pink and rose blossoms
set against deep green leaves...

...unexpected joy!

Joy is:
        the breeze caressing
            the skin   .
        peacefully whispering past,
          surrounding, enfolding

            ...blissful joy!

Joy is:
        knowing you do not have to be perfect,
            only trying to do the right thing.
        Being appreciated by God,
           loved for who you are...

           ...hopeful joy!

Chapter One
Creative Joy
(Joy in Discovery)

W*hat is your* dance *of life?*

To dance through life
we must listen to the
music within.
—Alan Fischer[1]

We each listen to a different music within, one
uniquely our own. A special joy is finding and refining
that creative spark which leads us to follow in rhythm to
the pace and tempo of our God-given talents.

As children our imaginations were boundless.

Our playful intelligence explored and discovered, dreamed and dared. Anything seemed possible! As long as no one said, "You cannot do it," we believed that we could. After a few mishaps, however, we began to realize that there were some limits to what we could safely do. And, we developed fear—fear of pain, fear of punishment, and the most devastating of all, fear of ridicule. For as Mister Rogers says, "Children long to belong,"[2] especially to be part of a family.

We learned as children to curtail our playful imaginations which sometimes led us to actions we later regretted. Not only had we proudly showed off our ideas and skills to our friends and family, but also to our teachers. But, wait, the art teacher said that I didn't draw the house right! She said it was too skinny and tall, but doesn't she know that's how it looks to me. I'm a little person and from way down here, the house looms up at me. My mother always said she liked my drawings and she used to put them on the refrigerator where she could enjoy them and everyone else could see them. I wish they would make up their minds! Well, maybe I just won't draw anymore if I can't please everyone. I used to really like to draw, too.

And, so it goes as our creativity becomes more and more constricted, our joy increasingly restricted.

My husband, Dave, is a crystallographer, a physical chemist who studies the structure of crystals within the body, especially in bones and teeth. Like many of us he is also fascinated with the wonderful crystal displays

all around us in nature such as frosty patterns on windowpanes and fanciful flakes of snow falling from the heavens.

Due to his crystallography background, Dave has always been interested in rocks and minerals. He has shared with me a special formation of rock called a geode. It often appears like a ball of solidified mud or clay ranging from a size easily held in the palm of your hand to a tubular form thirty or more feet long. If it is split open it reveals a wonderful treasure of crystals within. He calls these "miniature crystal caves," and the crystals can be clear quartz, purple amethysts, or any of a number of other beautiful minerals. No one can be certain exactly what is inside a geode until someone takes a chance and breaks it open, but it can be a joyous sight of surprising beauty. As adults, our creative selves have often been encrusted by doubt over the years, burying our talents within. Breaking through these tough outer layers is taking a chance, for finding our *real selves* so long hidden comes with no guarantees. But, among the many facets of our lives are at least some surprisingly beautiful surfaces. Opening ourselves to the light of Christ reflects those creative sparks of our interior "crystal caves."

> I want the light
> locked inside to awaken:
>   crystalline flower,
>   wake as I do:

eyelids raise the curtain
of endless earthen time
until deeply buried eyes
flash clear enough again
to see their own clarity.
—Pablo Neruda[3]

Allow yourself to marvel at the beauty of your true essence. Be patient, as the creative you unfolds. Feel the joy of newness, and yet remembered freedom, flow through and around you. Experience the wonder of this discovery as it evolves. For as Sam Keen wrote in *To a Dancing God*, ancient philosophers insisted that the "attitude of wonder...was the prerequisite for all wisdom."[4]

The world of wonder evolves from our ability to be surprised or amazed—to appreciate the miracle within a tiny bud, imagining it as it will soon become, or viewing it blossoming in seconds in astonishing time-lapse photography. We can be awed by the grandeur of the heavens' starry display on a clear night. And we can stare fascinated at the intricate patterns of color and form on the tiniest insect reflected in the light near the door as we return home that same night.

Little and Large
Lord,
    You have created
        the baby and the adult—
        the sapling and the full tree—

the minute and the aeon—
the drop and the flood.
But also, Lord,
You have created
the hummingbird and the ostrich—
the chipmunk and the dinosaur—
the grass blade and the sequoia—
the atom and the solar system.
How revealing, Lord, that not all little must
become large.
If my little is as much as intended, Lord, use it!
If my large has become what it should, use it!
Give me confidence to know my own littles
and larges.

—James J. Overholt[5]

We pray that we will have the strength to explore the miracles that are within us regardless of their size. We ask for openness to appreciate new perspectives. For "creativity comes from looking for the unexpected and stepping outside your own experience.[6]

God has blessed us with the power of imagination to see life and glimpse its truth in many different ways. Cheryl Forbes sees imagination as "the *imago Dei* in us. It helps us to know God, receive his grace, worship him, and see life through his eyes."[7] C. S. Lewis understands imagination as "the organ of meaning,"[8] while Robert J. Wicks speaks of "hope-infused images," for "with hope, imaging ourselves and the world becomes an invitation to see God in different ways."[9]

As we allow ourselves to imagine and create, let us remember that we are being newly created in the process. Our lives are the greatest works of art!

Chapter Two
Faith Joy
(Gifts Unfolding)

*F*aith is the bird
that feels the light
and sings when
the dawn is still dark.
                    —Rabindranath Tagore[1]

Faith is the willingness to let go and allow God
to fill us, and move us in the paths he has so chosen,
even when we cannot see where the road leads.

The true evidence of God in our lives is to see
the gifts of the Spirit flourishing in and around us. We
are each given at least one gift. However, we must open
ourselves to God in order to receive these gifts. "Now

there are diversities of gifts, but the same Spirit" (1 Cor. 12:4, King James Version [KJV]).

"God has given each of us the ability to do certain things well. So if God has given you the ability to prophesy, then prophesy whenever you can—as often as your faith is strong enough to receive a message from God. If your gift is that of serving others, serve them well" (Rom. 12:6-7, LB).

We need also to be open to the fruits of the Spirit, for Gods wants us to have full measure of "Love, *joy*, peace, patience, kindness, goodness, faithfulness, gentleness, self-control" (Gal. 5:22, RSV). We need to appreciate and seek to fulfill the measure of each Spirit-filled gift we have been given. Let it show!

Upon receiving these gifts one is filled with joy. Join God's joyful dance of faith! Joy is a grace given in love by God releasing the love from within ourselves. We have faith that even beneath the snow, there are flowers that will bloom in the spring. And, lo, the crocuses begin to show their colorful blossoms while there is yet snow. We have joy because of the faith in God's presence within us which will melt an icy heart, revealing the blossoming joy emerging.

> Let my love like sunlight
> surround you, yet give you
> illumined freedom.
> —Rabindranath Tagore[2]

The joy of our faith develops partly from the trust that God will be there for us when we need support and guidance in our lives. This gives us hope for today as well as tomorrow.

> The natural flights of the human mind are not from pleasure to pleasure but from hope to hope.
> —Samuel Johnson[3]

Whether we are grieving over the loss of someone we love, or are struggling against the constraints that bind us, God is there if only we would reach out. We have the hope that God can and will help in times when the problems become too great to bear. Hannah Whitall Smith says that Christians do bring their troubles to God, but the problem is, they do not always leave them there.

"The greatest burden we have to carry in life is self.... In laying off your burdens, therefore, the first one you must get rid of is yourself. You must hand yourself, with your temptations, your temperament, your frames and feelings, and all your inward and outward experiences, over into the care and keeping of your God, and leave it all there."[4]

Perhaps we are not willing to rely on God's timing, when the answer to our concern is not immediately forthcoming. Significant changes cannot be rushed and usually involve conflict and struggle. As Billy Graham states, "Comfort and prosperity have never enriched the world as much as adversity has. Out of pain and problems

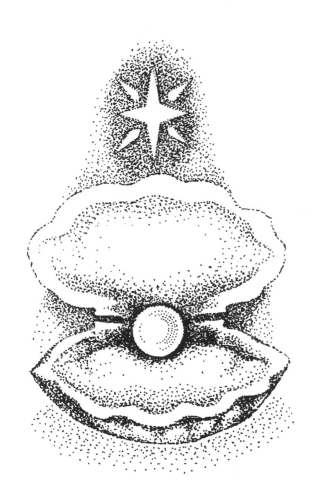

have come the sweetest songs, and the most gripping stories."[5] And God gives us many beautiful examples of this in nature, including majestic mountains, sandy beaches, and lustrous pearls, all born of forces in conflict.

The Pearl

> The pearl that you are
> is better by far
> than the brightest star,
> the costliest gem ...
> for costly it has been.
> —*Beverly Elaine Eanes*

Our lives are full of irritants which, if we try to ignore them, will simply fester. If we learn to limit them, polishing them and setting guidelines within the scope of our possibilities, we will give ourselves time to allow the surfaces to shine with increased luster.

> The art of life
> lies in constant
> readjustment
> to our surroundings.
> —Okakura Kakuzo[6]

Part of this readjustment must be a change in our attitude, and this comes from viewing our world from a different perspective. Robert J. Wicks sees perspective as "the cornerstone of spiritual and psychological health."[7] He goes on to say that it is not our environment that is the key, but how we put up with it.

> Attitudes are more important than facts!
> —Karl Menninger[8]

As a Jew, Dr. Viktor Frankl was imprisoned by the Nazis, and all the members of his family were killed. In addition to his freedom, even his clothes and his wedding ring were taken from him. His words belied the depths of misfortune and gave voice to his amazing attitude and incredible power of perspective, for he said: there is "one thing no person can ever take away from me—and that is my freedom to choose how I will react to what happens to me!"[9]

God is there to help us with our 'attitude adjustment' again and again. We don't always believe that we can handle another problem or learn to modify our view of it so that we can choose how to react to it. But God has a plan for each of our lives, and we must be ready to search for the path and to leap from rock to rock across the stream of adversity without fearing the occasional splash. Not fearing to fall, one is able to leap with abandon as does the dancer, with "an energy and fearlessness that is essential to excitement."[10]

> ...so that I might finish my course with joy
> (Acts 20:24, KJV).

We need to leap with faith, to feel the excitement and joy as we are released from fear. And we need to share that joy of faith not only with others, but with our creator who delights in our joy. Lord, remind me to include you in my joys—not just to call out to you in my anguish!

Let us take hold in faith and joy that which God would have us do. In the words of Oswald Chambers, "Joy means the perfect fulfillment of that for which I was created.... We have all to find our niche in life, and spiritually we find it when we receive our ministry from the Lord."[11]

> You have come here
> to find what you
>   already have.
> —Buddhist Aphorism[12]

Chapter Three

Healing Joy
(Joy in Letting Go)

H*e that lives in hope dances without music.*
*   —George Herbert[1]*

Try dancing with a millstone around your neck! It
sounds more than a bit awkward—it seems almost impossible, and certainly not worth the effort. The body would be
weighted down with the effort and it would even be difficult to keep one's balance, much less dance. There would
be no thought of the precision and timing, let alone the
free floating movement of creative expression.

Who would suggest such a thing? It sounds so
incongruous! Would it surprise you to know that you
have danced this way many times in your life? No, it is

not a reflection on your dancing skill or lack thereof. You are free to dance in your own way and to whatever beat you hear. However, even the most skilled and talented ballet dancer will have difficulty executing fundamental movements when confined by a "millstone mentality." This is the term used by Norman Vincent Peale when speaking of people who are focusing on past disappointments which weigh them down like a millstone around their neck, "draining their energy, holding them back." He writes of this phenomenon in an article called, "A Word You Can Do Without."[2] The word he would like us to do without is *regret*. We know that it is difficult to see the road ahead when we keep looking over our shoulders. And yet, we wish that things could have been different. 'If only....' These two words alone speak eloquently of our regret, and each time they are thought or spoken they drag us down. Robert Schuller's prescription "is to strike those words from your life! Replace them with the words, 'next time.' Do not deny the reality of mistakes made or sins committed, but learn to forgive yourself."[3]

God truly delights in us as his special creation! Yes, he knows we are not perfect, we make human mistakes, and we sometimes have peculiar ideas and habits. He created us as human just as his Son, Jesus, was sent in earthly form that he might better understand us and our many needs. Christ came to close the distance from human to God. Christ showed us how God can right our human wrongs, and gave us the ultimate example of forgiveness.

What is life like when we are unable to forgive? As Robert Schuller states, "It is impossible to have thoughts of resentment and jealousy, anger and hate and ill-will—and be happy. You cannot sow these negative emotional seeds and expect to raise a harvest of smiles and laughter. Nobody can be happy and bitter at the same time."[4]

Do not let the person who has offended you hurt you further by stirring your defenses in an attempt to protect yourself. Rationally this makes sense, but once emotions are stirred, actions and reactions are not always predictable. Eventually, bitterness turned outward simply turns inward and eats away at our peace and happiness. Do not chew on the bitterness within you for it will color your whole world...you will see the world through bile-colored glasses.

> Hate is a prolonged form of suicide.
> —Johann Friedrich von Schiller[5]

Forgiveness can be transcendent, for there is joy in the release of resentment and anguish. Forgiveness makes healing possible as illustrated in this story told by Elton Trueblood. An unforgiving "man, who had not been able to walk a city block for years, and who had subjected himself to the ministrations of many healers, walked out of the pastor's study...and walked immediately for twenty blocks... He found something on his knees that he had never found anywhere else."[6]

> Write injuries in sand,
> kindnesses in marble.[7]
> —French proverb

Forgiveness is God's great gift. Can we *accept* it *and share* it? We must first truly believe that God forgives us, and does so without reservation. Man finds it difficult to believe that such love is possible in view of all of his sins. It is difficult enough for us to believe that God so loves and forgives us, but harder still to believe that another person could be forgiving. We are certainly mysteries to each other. Seemingly the most difficult aspect to fathom is the ability to forgive oneself. And here is the most significant mystery, the inner self. But, if we are created in God's image, we must be lovable. Why, then, are we so hard on ourselves? God is waiting for us to grab hold of his wonderful forgiveness model. When we can harness our "fire for change," our "passion for justice" which Sr. Maureen McCann calls the "anger which unites us," she says that we will know the depth of God's desire for our self-forgiveness. If God desires it with such passion, who are we to deny that forgiveness for ourselves?[8]

Forgiveness is a risk, it is love's daring response. God has shown us this way to love one another.

The Darker Side of Light

> Hidden beneath the mask
> of light and joy—

resentment and bitterness
        lurking, ready
        to make a move—
Someone stealing
        what's rightfully ours.
Deserving a chance, a raise,
        a friend;
Others keep us from
        our 'just desserts'
Fair? No!
But,
        Letting go....
        The only hope.
        —Beverly Elaine Eanes

Who is suffering the most? We smugly like to think that we are the righteous ones who have been harmed, and therefore will make the other person suffer for it by not forgiving them. The other person may be hurt, but *we* suffer the most. It's hard to keep warm wrapped in righteous indignation, and we certainly don't appear warm and fuzzy to anyone else. It's not fun for others to be around us, and after a while it's not fun to live with ourselves. The only things which germinate from righteous indignation are pinched nostrils, compressed lips, a stony heart, and a lack of laugh crinkles around the eyes.

How can we not only forgive others, but also do it graciously? Understanding is the key to unlocking your stony heart. People don't always mean to hurt us. Even when they do, "they know not what they do," as Christ said to his Father when on the cross. He wanted God to forgive those who had physically and mentally tortured him. Those who harm others are very troubled people. This does not excuse their actions, but it helps in our understanding. Forgiving them, as Robert Schuller says, "we move from the defensive to the offensive.... We become compatible instead of combatable."[9] This does not mean that we are able to forget what has happened to us, because forgiving someone does not condone the act. Instead of thinking "forgive and forget," Sharon Cheston suggests we use the phrase "remit and omit." *Remit* not only means to forgive, but also "to refrain from exacting payment and to submit for judgment or action to someone whose business it is to look after such things. *Omit* means to leave out" and involves conscious ability unlike the idea of forgetting which seems almost impossible, at times. Cheston believes that one "does not need to forget, but rather consciously to omit the information or pain from determining" our future.[10]

We are forgiving the *person* and sharing the forgiveness model which Christ taught us. If you have been so severely harmed that you can not forgive at this time, ask God to do it for you, and ask that God give you strength to forgive in time. The danger is waiting too long, as Anne Morrow Lindbergh describes in a case of a woman who was dying. "She said not 'good-bye' but 'forgive me'...the two words (in Russian) are practically interchangeable! It is the profoundest, the last good-bye."[11]

The understanding may come later, but the decision to forgive needs to come now. Separate the decision from the feelings while there is still time for both of you. However, even after the other person's death you can still write a letter of reconciliation which you can read in privacy at the graveside, or be of help to the family in some way. Unburden your heart today!

And what of the often not mentioned problem of forgiving God? We think he should stop us from ever making mistakes. We think he should not take away loved ones even unto himself. It's unlikely that God is responsible for these tragedies, but we must blame someone. Because we dare not hate God, we hate his world and ourselves as well. Lewis B. Smedes says that "Hating God's most precious gift is a believer's sneaky way to hate God."[12] It is essential that we bring forth this pain and anger so that it will not continue to turn inward, causing us even more harm. God knows that we will blame him for disasters not of our own making, nor of his. He understands when we rail against him. He wants only for us to understand that when calamity strikes he is there for us offering strength and support.

"Letting go" by forgiving...the freedom brings great joy!

> On with the dance!
> let joy be unconfined.
> —Byron[13]

Chapter Four

Now Joy
(Moving in the Moment)

I *think the reason dance has held such an ageless magic for the world is that it has been the symbol of the performance of living.*

—Martha Graham[1]

Dance allows the person to be in the present moment, imprinting the message being portrayed, instilling the message in the here and now. And yet dance can transport the body and the soul of the participant and often the viewer alike beyond the boundaries of space and time. Even the imprisoned body forced to restrict movement through illness, or age, or the vagaries of war can move beyond the confines of the body's shell. Many a prisoner of war has saved his sanity by moving through his imagination beyond the walls surrounding him. Several years ago, I was studying sacred dance. One of my classmates was a woman in a wheelchair, whose movements were limited mainly to those above the waist. No one in the class was more enthusiastic or more inspiring in worship through movement than was she. It showed in the glow on her face, the outstretched arms, and the adoring hands. The word of God becomes embedded in movement and flows forth in worship and love.

> The body must not stand in the way
> of the soul's expression.
> —La Méri[2]

Many years ago, as a member of Faith United Methodist Church in Rockville, Maryland, I formed a sacred dance group. I called the group "Faith in Motion." It was a nice play on words, of course, but the name meant much more than that, for truly the movements were inspired by the faith within reaching out in adoration and love. Many of the movement motifs, or dance patterns, had symbolic meaning, and no words were needed to explain them: the sheltering arm, the bent knee, the bowed head, or the leaping for joy! I have always felt closest to God in adoration through movement and music. When I was born, I had severely bowed legs and the doctor's prescription to my mother was a prophetic one: "Massage her legs every day, and when she can walk she should study ballet." God must have sent this healer who used these more natural methods, for I was not only spared braces, but I discovered a wonderful new world. This world of dance eventually led to joyous celebration and adoration of God.

> BACH gave us God's Word
> MOZART gave us God's Laughter
> BEETHOVEN gave us God's Fire
> ## GOD
> gave us MUSIC that we
> might pray without words
> —from a German Opera House[3]

Many pilgrims move with only the internal music of their love and piety—they walk or crawl often over difficult terrain to their holy places. This movement of adoration may take weeks, and the culmination as they reach the holy place brings smiles mixed with tears. Their faith had sustained them as they moved minute by minute to their goal.

> God never asks about our
> ability or inability—
> just about our availability.
> —Anonymous[4]

Joy is looking inward with love—a new outlook and a new inlook. Joy is opening your heart to compassion for *your self*. Joy is appreciating God's delight in what he sees in you.

> Joy is not in things; it is in us.
> —Richard Wagner[5]

Feel the beauty inside you as with all of God's creation which moves and swirls around you. Feel yourself frolicking as a frisky colt in spring kicking up his heels and romping with joy and abandon!

> Grace is the courage to be at home in the moving resonance of the present.
>
> —Sam Keen[6]

If there is something that you want to do in your life, but have been restrained for some reason, seize it—let it flow. As Robert Schuller says, "Your dream is God within you!"[7] Appreciate the vistas of joy, the dancing designs of nature, but remember the internal beauty within you and others that reflects God's image. Discover newness, but savor tradition; appreciate order, but recognize that chaos may bring necessary change.

> All things are connected like the blood that unites us. Man did not weave the web of life, he is merely a strand in it. Whatever he does to the web, he does to himself.
>
> —attributed to Chief Seattle[8]

We are part of an incredibly intricate system where every movement has meaning. Move out with joy and integrity into the fullness of life as God intended. Live in the moment with the joy of God's presence and remember God's promise to unite us all in the future.

May
our beautiful Lord
give you
an
unexpected surprise
of joy
before
every sunset
of your
life!
—Robert Schuller[9]

Chapter Five
Shared Joy
(Playing with Possibilities)

*I*t's a happy
talent
To know how
to play.

–Ralph Waldo Emerson[1]

Years ago I heard someone talking about "choosing God's foolishness." That seemed a little strange as I had always thought of God as having serious intent. After all, he had tremendous responsibility, didn't he?

And then I saw a film about penguins. Talk about foolishness! They have even caused controversy as to whether they are birds, a separate superorder of their own, or descended from reptiles, as it appears that their ancestors never flew. That debate seems to have been settled and they are considered to be birds.[2] Beyond that decision, however, there still seems to be a design problem—at least at first glance.

Upright, on land, they seem stiff and awkward and can barely waddle. They're even dressed in what we think of as formal and stiff attire in their black and white tuxedos. Some species hop for short distances when they need to move upward on an incline of small rocks to their nests. However, the "fun" begins when they plop down in "bellyflop" position and "toboggan" from place to place on ice and snow. Not only is it a smooth and efficient form of land transportation, but it looks like simple joy as well. As they leap or jump into the cold sea, the true beauty of the penguin's seemingly "foolish" design becomes apparent. When searching for food, they move underwater like slick, swift, and sure torpedoes. They also "porpoise"—leaping and diving alternately. Porpoises, and some seals, have mastered this technique, but penguins are the only swimming birds who have adapted this maneuver. It must be efficient as they move very quickly through the water while still getting air, but it certainly looks like "play." Then, just as quickly, at fast speed, they can leap out of the water onto overhanging cliffs. Pretty amazing athletic prowess up to now, but again they waddle home like a short-stepping, time-delayed marching band.

Their duties at home are as impressive as their modes of transportation, for the usually monogamous

pair share the care of the young. For three weeks, the female stays at the site until she lays her egg or two in a nest which the male helped fashion and defend for her. He then incubates the unhatched egg on his feet covering it with his brood pouch. The male may go as long as five or six weeks from the time he first leaves the sea, settles his territory, mates, and incubates the egg. The mother takes off as soon as he begins to incubate the egg in order to feed in the sea to replenish her depleted stores of nourishment. Only after the penguin chick is born does the male return to the sea for his nourishment while she stays with the chick. This shared housekeeping and parenting is a model well ahead of its time.

If this is an example of God's foolishness, how marvelous! How lucky for us that we are able to share this wonderful whimsy of God.

Speaking of whimsy, play with your own imagination as if you were able to observe the beginning of creation. Picture God, with the whole world to fashion in any way he chooses and with no one to say how he's allowed to do it. Consider the infinite possibilities! Observe the joy surrounding the dashing designs of color and shape, texture and movement. And then wonder at the formation of fascinating creatures from single cell to billions of cells.

> The most prominent image of God in Genesis is movement.... Creation emerged—increasing, yielding and bursting forth. God fills creation and it

flies, creeps, sprouts up and grows. God breathes
and creation lives.

—Laura Hembree[3]

It doesn't matter how long all of this takes for
time is not a consideration. Who has a right to hurry
God? It is the process that matters, the art of creation for
beauty's sake. But the structure and function are incredible as well. Consider the intricate interrelationships, the
delicate balance and flow of all parts of this remarkable
system.

> We are part of a creative destiny,
> reaching backward and forward to infinity—
> a destiny that reveals itself, though dimly,
> in our striving, in our love,
> our thought, our appreciation.
>
> —J.E. Boodin[4]

God invites us to play, to let our creative imagination take us anywhere we choose. Experiencing joy along
the way can be like magic—appearing when least expected.
And the magic expands when the journeys of joy are
shared.

> To find joy
>   in another's joy
>   that is the secret
>   of happiness.
> —George Bernanos[5]

Touch the essence of someone's spirit with your own, for there lies the deepest happiness. Pass on the joy which you have experienced.

> Sow the seeds of happiness in others,
> and you will reap a joyful harvest.
> —Dr. Forrest C. Shaklee, Sr.[6]

When you accept people and don't judge them, you bring them joy at the outset. When you later share your own secret joys, you have made a special friend. Oswald Chambers asks if we have "ever let God tell us any of His joys...?"[7] I believe we do that when we appreciate and care for the world that he has made—when we stop to smell the rose, and share the beauty of new discoveries with others.

The fullness of shared joy may expand the experience of pain and loss and sorrow. C. S. Lewis speaks of his own experience when even in the sorrow of his wife's impending death, their sharing brought joy. "Many bad spots in our best times, many good ones in our worst.... It is incredible how much happiness, even how much gaiety, we sometimes had together after all hope was gone. How long, how tranquilly, how nourishingly, we talked together that last night!"[8]

> All men are one at the wellspring of pain and joy.
> —Henri Nouwen[9]

When the pretense is no longer necessary, even

time can take on special meaning. We can enjoy the life we are given to the fullest. Norman Cousins says, "Far more real than the ticking of time is the way we open up the minutes and invest them with meaning. Death is not the ultimate tragedy in life. The ultimate tragedy is to die without discovering the possibilities of full growth."[10]

And those possibilities are endless, even laughing oneself back to health, which was part of the prescription that Norman Cousins gave to himself. Toni Morrison believes, "You repossess your life when you laugh at the things that try to destroy you."[11]

We have seen that our God is playful, appreciates laughter, and shares his joy.

> Thou wilt show me the path of life:
> in thy presence is fullness of joy;
> at thy right hand there are pleasures for evermore.
> —Psalm 16:11, KJV

Playfulness is considered a gift from heaven. When does play begin? It probably begins as far back as the womb. There in the warmth and security of that cushioned chamber, the fetus is being nourished with oxygen and other nutrients, and rocked by the natural movements of the mother's body. And, suddenly, the mother is laughing delightedly, perhaps at the first movement of her fetus. Her laugh is a wonderful response to what is perhaps just a random movement of the fetus. But the delight keeps recurring with each movement felt by the mother, and each time blood moves more smoothly through the uterine vessels, bringing increased oxygen, followed by peace and relaxation. Later, when the small parts of the fetus are seen moving on her abdomen, both parents touch that area and wait for the fetus to respond with another similar movement. The parents are laughing at this wonderful new game of getting to know their unborn child. Play and laughter must be something special to look forward to on the outside; perhaps leaving this cushioned chamber will not be so scary after all. After the birth, play becomes crucial and it will develop as a natural phenomenon as long as the parent is responsive and the child continues to feel secure. Safe in the parent's arms the child reaches out and explores. Joseph Chilton Pearce talks about the importance of play, and he calls it the "over-arching intelligence" from which all the other intelligences develop.[12]

We also see the importance of play in many fields of endeavor. Authors and poets play with words to create pictures and stories, artists play with color and light and texture. Mathematicians play with number combinations, and scientists and philosophers play with ideas and concepts. Kary Mullis, who recently won the Nobel Prize for his extraordinary genetics research, says that "striking advances" in really good science come from "being playful."[13] Again, we are back to perspective, stepping outside of the usual and seeing something that was there all the time, but hidden by the well-ordered path taken everyday. We must not be afraid to step off the path.

One does not discover
new lands without consenting
to lose sight of the shore....
    —André Gide[14]

And what would play be without humor and laughter?

Humor is about perspective—
a willingness to access joy
even in adversity.
    —C. W. Metcalf[15]

The above quote comes from Anne Wilson Schaef's book, *Laugh, I Thought I'd Die (If I Didn't)*. She herself says, "I realize that humor isn't for everyone. It's only for people who want to have fun, enjoy life, and feel alive."[16] She also has written a delightful prayer, "May I open myself this day to the chuckle within, the giggle without, and the laughter and joy that are everywhere."[17]

There are many things in life that elicit humor. And while laughing from seeing the different slant or the funny side of something, we are performing wonderful aerobics from the inside out. However, the most important perspective or slant is the one we take toward ourselves.

A sense of humor...
is the ability to understand a joke
...and the joke is oneself.
    —Clifton Fadiman[18]

Angels fly because they take themselves lightly.

—G. K. Chesterton[19]

When we begin to take ourselves too seriously, we are often expecting perfection. This means we allow ourselves no mistakes—not even silly ones. Now, we know that humans can be pretty ridiculous, especially when we are trying to do so many things as part of a fast-paced lifestyle. Silly things also happen when our memory evades us as we mature chronologically. Just last week, I found three shriveled looking baked potatoes in the oven. I had baked the potatoes three nights before, but left them in the oven to keep them warm while waiting for my husband to come home that night. Needless to say, they were no longer warm. And I laugh at the sight of penguin antics!

When we can view ourselves as one of God's creatures to whom he has given many abilities and much responsibility, but also the gift of chuckling at our absurdities, we will be at peace with ourselves. There is much joy in this peace.

> The little cares that
> fretted me,
> I lost them yesterday,
> Among the fields above
> the sea,
> Among the winds
> at play...
>
> —Elizabeth Barrett Browning[20]

May you appreciate the unfolding of your creative joy as your imagination soars. May you leap for joy with faith in God's timing, and with some of his perspective. May you let go of the bitterness, and allow forgiveness to graciously fill your life. May you experience joy in the moment, and move forth with the word of God. May playfulness infuse the serious purpose of your life. And may you share the joy of that play and laughter so that others, too, might find happiness.

Remember that dancing transcends who you are in the everyday.

> There is only the dance.
> —T. S. Eliot[21]

Your dance matters, why not share the joy of it?

Sharing God's Joy

> Joy is a name
> a dance
> a spirit
> to be;
> free
> in harmony
> with God's
> magic music
> moving
> all around us.
> —*Beverly Elaine Eanes*

Chapter Six
Unending Joy
(Transformation in Mystery)

Most people seem very desirous of heaven—someday. But to die for it, that's another story!

Our lives are filled with unknowns: Who will get the promotion, or, worse, who will be laid off? Have I studied enough for this exam, or, worse, did I study the right things? Is this lump benign, or is it cancer that has already spread? And, what of the final unknown, death? Will it be painful or scary, and will we know that it is time to let go? If we do, indeed, die alone, will God truly be waiting to greet us? And will we again see all of our loved ones who have gone before us?

> Whether we live or whether we die, we are the Lord's.
>
> —Rom. 14:8, RSV

For true joy in this life, there must be meaning in it. We as a society need to be more concerned with how individual people have lived—how meaningful their life has been, not how much power or wealth they have accumulated.

We each deal with limitations in our lives: skills that could be sharper, talents we wish we possessed, and beauty which is elusive. Some limitations are physical, others are psychological or spiritual. As we age, there are losses which compound these limitations, especially in the realm of memory and physical prowess. And, as time goes by, we lose more and more of our loved ones which limits our support structure when we need it most.

With our increasing awareness of our limitations and losses comes the need to let go our tenacious hold of who we think we need to be, both within our own eyes, and in the sight of the world. We truly must let God take our brokenness and help to redesign our attitude. Knowing that God loves us with all of our limitations, we can finally appreciate each person as a unique and blessed creation. As Maxie Dunham states, "the real test of a man as he faces life is whether he runs, fights, whimpers or **dances**."[1] For pain as well as beauty comes into the lives of each one of us. Increasingly though, to balance the pain, we must reach toward beauty to sustain ourselves as well as those around us.

As we reach out toward the beauty we see in others, we can appreciate ourselves more as well. Charles Swindoll speaks about people who are able to give affirmations to others as showing an important sign of maturity. We must give the affirmation to people personally, for who they are, not just in gratitude for what they have done.[2]

Sue Monk Kidd states that there is "not a moment to spare," for the time to love is short. She is speaking about lost relationships and how important it is to heal old wounds.[3] The person who has injured us may die without us coming together for one last time. Reaching out to heal lost relationships requires a big heart, which not only accepts but embraces the person, foibles and all. This helps to ease the hurt and lead toward a much needed reconciliation. We each need to do our part to preserve life and loving relationships. Albert Schweitzer states it thus:

> The small amount you are able to do is actually much if it only relieves pain, suffering, and fear from any living being be it human or any other creature. The preservation of life is the true joy.

He goes on to say that this service of love in an imperfect world "forms a preparatory stage to the bliss that awaits [us] in the perfected world, the Kingdom of God."[4]

Our world on earth, of course, is not perfect though we strive to do the right things. We make human mistakes which cannot be undone; they can only hope to be rectified at best. We must trust that the Lord understands our sincere intentions for good and forgives us when our feet stray from the path. When we have lived a

meaningful, though not perfect life, we may go to our maker in joy. There is joy in the life well-lived coming to an end here on earth—this ending, too, is newness and discovery and hope for the future.

A long life, lived well, makes the leaving of this world easier for ourselves and our loved ones. But, what of the death of a small child? The life of a small child or even of a fetus coming to an end too soon still has meaning. Parents mourn what might have been—the unfulfilled hopes and unrealized dreams. A child's life, at any age, can be an intense joy though compacted in time. Even knowing that a child is expected can bring joy in anticipation. Far more difficult to understand is why some children who die young must deal with the pains and anxieties of such dreaded diseases as leukemia. For those children, not able to be cured, their lives may be a real struggle in the difficult last months. Even this last struggle may, nevertheless, have meaning in the courage shown— the brave smile, the tolerance for more tests or treatments, and the final letting go.

> Blessed are the pure in heart
> for they shall see God.
> —Matt. 5:8 (RSV)

Even though they will not fully understand the unfairness of losing a little one, the parents may one day be sustained by the joy, though all too brief, that their child brought them. Even a caterpillar must struggle at what appears to be the end of its life. But we know that struggle will lead to a new life and that a butterfly will be born to dance in glory. We can also take joy, then, in knowing that the child will be born again in the heart of God.

With meaning in our lives, we are ever evolving toward our creator. God's joy embraces us, and there is room for all in God's heart. Professor John Polkinghorne speaks of "God the Creator, the One who holds the world in being. Creation is not an act of the remote past but a continuing act of the divine will in every present moment."[5] And, as a part of this vast universe, we are of this world each day and inextricably of God forever as a part of the earth and beyond. Teilhard de Chardin saw the joy and strength of his life when he realized that bringing God and the world together "set up an endless mutual reaction, producing a sudden blaze of such intense brilliance that all the depths of the world were lit up for me."[6]

Matter and spirit exist together in a confluence of wholeness and holiness. At death we are not just taken to the Lord, but we continue to develop that relationship more fully in another realm.

> The only thing you lose is something you don't need anymore...your physical body. It's like putting away your winter coat when spring comes.
> —Elisabeth Kübler-Ross[7]

How do we, in fact, trust that this relationship

continues after our earthly death? It is, after all, the *ultimate* trust! We have been developing our ability to trust since we were born (perhaps even before) when we needed complete caretaking for our safety and security. However, even parents who are trying hard, make mistakes—they don't always follow through when they say they will do something, or they yell more than necessary because they are tired, and therefore our trust is tested. Some children, whose parents are, for whatever reason, unreliable, lose all ability to trust. Also, as we grow up, we encounter many types of people, and we learn that not all of them are trustworthy. Is it not understandable, then, that regardless of our general degree of trust, we may find it even more difficult to trust in the unknown? Even during a lifetime of relating to God, there is still that final leap of faith.

The fetus may be reluctant to leave the warmth and known world of the womb. The reality of the world after birth may be a scary place, but then the child and later the adult discovers how exciting and meaningful a place it can be and then does not want to leave this known world. Once that last leap into the unknown is made, Norman Vincent Peale says, "he will once again feel loving arms beneath him and once again look up into a strong, beautiful face," and want to remain there.[8]

On the brink of our transformation from this earth to new life, we are searching the hidden places of our souls. We must bring to God who we really are without regrets or excuses. There is no room for rationalizations about our past behavior. God knows the essence of our heart in our loving and caring relationships, be they human or divine. God accepts where we are when we are approaching death. Ron James describes what it must have been like for St. Paul when he was in prison and facing death. "He stands at the limit of this mortal life, as it were, curls his toes over the edge of the mystery, and feels the mist in his face and the fog in his throat."[9]

In our final trust, we move forward into this great mystery, which cannot be solved by mere mortals, knowing that we need the power of God to sustain us. We must have hope and confidence born from God's love that has been caring for us here on earth. We must remember the sparkle of the night sky, the shimmer on sun-danced waters, and anticipate the indescribable joy that awaits us. For, if God could fashion such beauty on the earth, there is no limit to the luminous rapture of joy and peace we will have in our eternal home.

> A thing of beauty is a joy forever:
> Its loveliness increases; it will
> never pass into nothingness.
> —John Keats[10]

Inspiring Joys
to carry with you...

Grief can take care of itself; but to get
the full value of joy you must have
someone to divide it with.

—Mark Twain[1]

* * *

She gives most who gives with joy.

—Mother Teresa[2]

* * *

Joy is the simplest form of gratitude.

—Karl Barth[3]

* * *

Where there is sadness,
　Let me sow joy....

—St. Francis of Assisi[4]

* * *

The journey is the joy.

—Robert J. Hastings[5]

* * *

There is no psychiatrist in the world like a puppy licking your face.

—Bern Williams[6]

* * *

Let them praise his name with dancing.

—Psalm 149:3 (RSV)

* * *

Your dance is never completed—
you will always be moving toward a new life.

ENJOY!

Notes

(References that are designated with the words "source unknown" have been attributed to the author so stated. Many resulted from seeing the quotation on a print or plaque.)

Introduction
    1. Vincent Harding and Rosemarie Freeney Harding, "Touching the Hem of the Garment," *Sojourners*, March, 1988, p. 33.

Chapter One. Creative Joy (Joy in Discovery)
    1. Alan Fischer, source unknown.
    2. Mr. Rogers, "Today Show," National Broadcasting Company, Feb. 19, 1993.
    3. Pablo Neruda, *Skystones XII*, 1970, source unknown.
    4. Sam Keen, *To a Dancing God*, New York: Harper and Row, Publishers, 1970, p. 43.
    5. James J. Overholt, *From Tiny Beginnings*, Elgin, Illinois: Brethren Press, 1987, p. 14.

6. Brenton R. Schlender, "Human Touch," from *Fortune* magazine, cited in "Personal Glimpses," *Reader's Digest*.

7. Cheryl Forbes, *Imagination: Embracing a Theology of Wonder*, Portland, Oregon: Multnomah Press, 1986, p. 18.

8. C. S. Lewis, source unknown.

9. Robert J. Wicks, *Living Simply in an Anxious World: An Invitation to Perspective*, New York: Paulist Press, 1988, p. 22.

Chapter Two. Faith Joy (Gifts Unfolding)

1. Rabindranath Tagore, source unknown.

2. Rabindranath Tagore, source unknown.

3. Samuel Johnson, cited in *Guideposts*, July, 1993, p. 9.

4. Hannah Whitall Smith, *The Christian's Secret of a Happy Life*, Westwood, N.J.: Barbour and Company, Inc., 1985, p. 18.

5. Billy Graham, *Reader's Digest*, Jan., 1993, p. 156.

6. Okakura Kakuzo, source unknown.

7. Robert J. Wicks, "Reaching Out Without Being Pulled Down," featured speaker, Psychiatric Institute of Montgomery County, June 12, 1991.

8. Karl Menninger, cited in Robert Schuller, *You Are Wonderful*, Waco, Texas: Word Books, 1987.

9. Viktor Frankl, cited in Robert Schuller, *The Be (Happy) Attitudes*, Waco, Texas: Word Books, 1985, p. 199.

10. Toni Bentley, cited in May Blake, *The Dance Notebook*. Philadelphia: Running Press Book Publishers, 1984.

11. Oswald Chambers, *My Utmost for His Highest*, New York: Dodd, Mead and Company, Inc., 1935, p. 65.

12. Buddhist Aphorism, source unknown.

Chapter Three. Healing Joy (Joy in Letting Go)

1. George Herbert, source unknown.

2. Norman Vincent Peale, "A Word You Can Do Without," *Guideposts*, June, 1991, p. 13.

3. Robert Schuller, *The Be (Happy) Attitudes*, Waco, Texas: Word Books, 1985.

4. Robert Schuller, *Here's Happiness*, Waco, Texas: Word Books, 1987.

5. Johann Friedrich von Schiller, cited in Lewis B. Smedes, *Forgive and Forget: Healing the Hurts We Don't Deserve*, New York: Simon and Schuster, Inc., 1984.

6. Elton Trueblood, *The Life We Prize*, New York: Harper and Brothers, Publishers, 1951, p. 207.

7. French proverb, source unknown.

8. Maureen McCann, *Free to Forgive*, The Modern Cassette Library, Notre Dame, Indiana: Ave Maria Press, 1989.

9. Robert Schuller, *The Be (Happy) Attitudes*, Waco, Texas: Word Books, 1985.

10. Sharon Cheston, "Counseling Adult Survivors of Childhood Sexual Abuse, *Clinical Handbook*

of Pastoral Counseling, vol. 2, Robert J. Wicks and Richard D. Parsons (eds.), 1993, p. 483.

11. Anne Morrow Lindbergh, cited in *A Rumor of Angels*, Gail Perry and Jill Perry (eds.), New York: Ballantine Books, 1989, p. 167.

12. Lewis B. Smedes, *Forgive and Forget: Healing the Hurts We Don't Deserve*, San Francisco: Harper and Row, Publishers, 1984.

13. Lord Byron, source unknown.

Chapter Four. Now Joy (Moving in the Moment)

1. Martha Graham, cited in Amy Blake, *The Dance Notebook*, Philadelphia: Running Press Book Publishers, 1984.

2. La Méri, source unknown.

3. From a German Opera House, source unknown.

4. Anonymous, source unknown.

5. Richard Wagner, source unknown.

6. Sam Keen, *To a Dancing God*, New York: Harper and Row, Publishers, 1970, p. 37.

7. Robert Schuller, *Here's Happiness*, Waco, Texas: Word Books, 1987.

8. Attributed to Chief Seattle, cited in "Why I've Gone to the Ends of the Earth," by Jacques d'Amboise, *Parade Magazine*, Oct. 17, 1993, p. 4.

9. Robert Schuller, *The Be (Happy) Attitudes*, Waco, Texas: Word Books, 1985.

Chapter Five. Shared Joy (Playing with Possibilities)

1. Ralph Waldo Emerson, source unknown.

2. Roger Tory Peterson, *Penguins*, Boston: Houghton Mifflin Company 1979, p. 3.

3. Laura Hembree, "Dancing to the Rhythm of Love," *The Disciple*, June, 1984, p. 15.

4. J.E. Boodin, source unknown.

5. George Bernanos, source unknown.

6. Forrest C. Shaklee, Sr., *Thoughtsmanship: Ten Rules for Happiness and Contentment*, San Francisco: Shaklee Corporation, 1951, p. 3.

7. Oswald Chambers, *My Utmost for His Highest*, New York: Dodd, Mead and Company, Inc., 1935, p. 155.

8. C. S. Lewis, cited in *A Rumor of Angels*, Gail Perry and Jill Perry (eds.), New York: Ballantine Books, 1989, p. 40.

9. Henri Nouwen, source unknown.

10. Norman Cousins, *Head First*, New York: Penguin Books, 1989, p. 5.

11. Toni Morrison, cited in *The Washington Post*, Oct. 10, 1993, p. B1.

12. Joseph Chilton Pearce, "The Magical Child," tape recording, Waldorf School Conference, Pinellas, Florida, Nov. 6, 1993.

13. Kary Mullis, "The Quirky Genius Who Is Changing Our World," by Jim Dwyer, *Parade Magazine*, Oct. 10, 1993, p. 8.

14. André Gide, cited in *A Rumor of Angels*, Gail

Perry and Jill Perry (eds.), New York: Ballantine Books, 1989, p. 171.

15. C. W. Metcalf, cited in Anne Wilson Schaef, *Laugh! I Thought I'd Die (If I Didn't)*, New York: Ballantine Books, 1990, p. xi.

16. Anne Wilson Schaef, *Laugh! I Thought I'd Die (If I Didn't)*, New York: Ballantine Books, 1990, Feb. 1.

17. Ibid., Jan. 2.

18. Clifton Fadiman, cited in Anne Wilson Schaef, *Laugh! I Thought I'd Die (If I Didn't)*, New York: Ballantine Books, 1990, Dec. 7.

19. G. K. Chesterton, cited in *Guideposts*, Carmel, New York: *Guideposts* Associates, Inc., Oct. 1993, p. 30.

20. Elizabeth Barrett Browning, source unknown.

21. T. S. Eliot, "Burnt Norton," in *Four Quartets*.

Chapter Six. Unending Joy (Transformation in Mystery)

1. Maxie Dunham, *Dancing at My Funeral*, Los Angeles: Action House, Publishers, 1976.

2. Charles Swindoll, "Have Fun as You Grow Up," *A Better Tomorrow*, Premiere Issue, 1993, p. 50.

3. Sue Monk Kidd, "Don't Let It End This Way," *A Better Tomorrow*, Premiere Issue, 1993, p. 87.

4. *Finding Our Place in the World, The Reflections of Albert Schweitzer*, Helen R. Neinast (ed.), Nashville: Upper Room Books, 1990, p. 38.

5. John Polkinghorne, in "The Scientists Who Believe in God," *Guideposts*, July, 1993, p. 40.

6. Pierre Teilhard de Chardin, *The Divine Milieu*, New York: Harper Colophon Books, Harper & Row, Publishers, 1968, p. 37.

7. Elisabeth Kübler-Ross, in *Notable Quotables*, compiled by Jerry Reedy, Chicago: World Book Encyclopedia, Inc., 1984, p. 7.

8. Norman Vincent Peale, *The Positive Power of Jesus Christ*, Wheaton, IL: Tyndale House Publishers, 1980.

9. Ron James, *A Joy Wider Than the World*, Nashville: Upper Room Books, 1992, p. 35.

10. John Keats, in *Notable Quotables*, compiled by Jerry Reedy, Chicago: World Book Encyclopedia, Inc., 1984, p. 5.

Inspiring Joys

1. Mark Twain, from *Pudd'nhead Wilson's New Calendar*, in *The Wit and Wisdom of Mark Twain*, Philadelphia: The Running Press in Miniature, 1990.

2. Mother Teresa of Calcutta, "Joy," *A Gift for God*, New York: Harper and Row, Publishers, 1975.

3. Karl Barth, source unknown.

4. St. Francis of Assisi, source unknown.

5. Robert J. Hastings, "The Station," *A Penny's Worth of Minced Ham*, Carbodale and Edwardsville, IL: Southern University Press, 1986, p. 91.

6. Bern Williams, source unknown.

ILLUMINATIONBOOKS

Other Books in the Series